CHINA
the land

Bobbie Kalman

A Bobbie Kalman Book

The Lands, Peoples, and Cultures Series

Crabtree Publishing Company
www.crabtreebooks.com

The Lands, Peoples, and Cultures Series

Created by Bobbie Kalman

For Caroline Walker
and Norman Endicott

Written by
Bobbie Kalman

Coordinating editor
Ellen Rodger

Editor
Jane Lewis

Editors/first edition
Janine Schaub
Christine Arthurs
Margaret Hoogeveen

Production coordinator
Rose Gowsell

Contributing editor
Lisa Gurusinghe

Production
Arlene Arch

Separations and film
Embassy Graphics

Printer
Worzalla Publishing Company

Map
Jim Chernishenko

Illustrations
Dianne Eastman: icons
David Wysotski, Allure Illustrations: back cover

Photographs
Jim Bryant: p. 10 (both), 19, 20, 21 (center); courtesy of the Consulate General of the People's Republic of China: p. 7; Dennis Cox/ChinaStock: p. 4-5, 9, 11 (top), 16 (right), 17 (inset), 26 (both), 27, 28; David Butz p. 14 (bottom); Ken Ginn/China Stock: p. 21 (bottom), 23; Xu Jiayan/China Stock: p. 30 (full page); Wolfgang Kaehler: p. 11 (bottom); Liu Liqun/ChinaStock: p. 24 (inset); Christopher Liu/ChinaStock: p. 8, 17 (top); Pat Morrow/First Light: p. 6, 18; courtesy of the Royal Ontario Museum: p. 12, 15; Ron Schroeder: p. 16 (left); Caroline Walker: p. 21 (top), 22, 30(inset); Xian Visual Arts Company: p. 29; Chen Yixin/ChinaStock: p. 25 (bottom); other images by Digital Stock

Every effort has been made to obtain the appropriate credit and full copyright clearance for all images in this book. Any oversights or omissions will be corrected in future editions.

Cover: The Great Wall of China has been a symbol of China for centuries. The massive man-made structure is visible from space

Title page: Farmers still practice ancient ways on many rice farms in China.

Back cover: The Giant Panda lives in the bamboo forests and mountain regions of southwestern China.

Published by
Crabtree Publishing Company

PMB 16A
350 Fifth Avenue
Suite 3308
New York
N.Y. 10118

612 Welland Avenue
St. Catharines
Ontario, Canada
L2M 5V6

73 Lime Walk
Headington
Oxford OX3 7AD
United Kingdom

Cataloging in Publication Data

Kalman, Bobbie
  China, the land / Bobbie Kalman. – Rev. ed.
    p.cm – (The lands, peoples, and cultures series)
  Includes index.
  ISBN 0-7787-9378-8 (RLB) -- ISBN 0-7787-9746-5 (pbk.)
    1. China–Description and travel–Juvenile literature. 2. China–History–Juvenile literature.[1. China.] I. Title. II Series.
  DS712 .K343 2001
  951–dc21   00-057080
                                                                   LC

Contents

4 The land of China

6 A land of many variations

11 The faces of China

12 China's early history

14 Political changes

16 A new way of life

18 Growing pains

20 Food for a billion!

22 Fishing

24 The cities of China

26 Transportation

28 The wonders of China

31 The Great Wall

32 Glossary and Index

The land of China

Over the centuries countless travelers have
journeyed to China and marveled at its ageless
treasures. Today, the country's vast landscape,
complex history, cultural events, and modern
cities fascinate millions of tourists every year.

How should we begin to talk about such a vast
country? When people describe the many
wonders of China, they often use superlatives.
Superlatives are words such as highest, biggest,
most, hottest, and longest.

A fascinating country

Of all the countries in the world, China has the most people. Over a billion people make China their home. China is the third biggest country, next to Russia and Canada. Its history dates back four thousand years, making China one of the oldest civilized countries. One of the world's hottest deserts is China's Taklamakan Desert.

The highest mountains in the world are the Himalayan mountains, found on the border between Tibet and Nepal. The tallest of these is Mount Everest. The Chinese Grand Canal is the longest canal in the world. The largest structure ever erected is the Great Wall of China. It winds through almost 3,729 miles (6000 km) of valleys and mountains.

A land of many variations

Travel across China, and you will be amazed at the variety of landscapes and range in **climates**. Take hiking boots and sandals, a warm coat, a bathing suit, an umbrella, and a water bottle. You will need them all!

The highest heights

China's geography can be divided into three areas according to their height above **sea level**. The first area, located in western China, is the highest. It includes enormous mountains and the largest plateau in the world, the Plateau of Tibet. A plateau is a flat, elevated area of land. Tibet is known as "the roof of the world" because its average height above sea level is 13,124 feet (4000 m). Tibet is a cold place! Its frost-free period is less than fifty days a year.

Mountains cover over one third of China's enormous land mass. The Himalayan Mountains are on the border of Tibet and Nepal. Mount Everest, the world's highest peak, is part of this range. This mountain, called *Qomolangma* by the Chinese, is 29,035 feet (8850 m) high and still grows about $2/5$ inch (1 cm) every two years as it continues to form!

Middle ground

The second area is not as high above sea level. It includes smaller mountain ranges and huge deserts. The Qilian Shan, the Qin Ling, and Kunlun Mountains are in this middle area. Two of China's main river systems, the Yellow (*Huang Ho*) and the Yangtze (*Chang Jiang*), originate in the heights of the Kunlun Mountains.

High and dry

To the northwest, the great mountain ranges enclose desert basins. One of these is the Taklamakan Desert. It is so hot in this region that raindrops evaporate before they touch the ground. Sandstorms last for days, and huge, shifting dunes seem to come to life as the wind shapes them.

(opposite) Mountain climbers attempt to scale Mount Everest, the world's highest peak.

The Gobi Desert is one of the world's biggest deserts. A large part of it is in the Mongolian area of northern China. Extreme temperatures are found within the vast area of the Gobi Desert. The temperature soars to 113°F (45°C) in some areas and, because of the northern location and high **altitude**, the temperature can also drop below -40°F (-40°C). Instead of sand, the Gobi desert is made up mostly of rock and gravel.

(below) Planting trees keeps the desert sands from overtaking the surrounding farmland.

The Wu Gorge on the Yangtze River is surrounded by cliffs that are 2,953 feet (900 m) high.

Coastal plains

On the last and lowest step are the coastal **plains**. These plains are just above sea level and extend along the coast of the South and East China Seas. This land is very **fertile**, and the weather is warm and wet. Ninety percent of China's population lives in these areas.

China's rivers

The two major rivers in China are the Yellow and the Yangtze Rivers. The Yellow River system is one of the world's major water highways. At 3,474 miles (5590 km) in length, the Yangtze is the fourth-longest river in the world. Its Chinese name, *Chang Jiang*, means "Great River." Both the Yangtze and Yellow rivers flow from the high western mountains to the lower eastern regions.

Flood waters: friend or foe?

Rivers are a source of life. Their waters provide riverside communities with fish, and their **silt** fertilizes the areas of land close to the water. The areas around the great rivers of China are huge, flat, fertile basins. The Yellow River basin, for example, is the most important flat land in China's northeast. The soil is rich and holds moisture well. It is ideal for agriculture.

As well as being a source of life, rivers can also be a source of disaster. The Chinese call the Yellow River "China's Sorrow." In the past three thousand years it has overflowed more than 1500 times, causing much damage and costing many lives. To control floods, the Chinese have built high banks of earth, called dikes, along the edges of their rivers.

Yu the Great

The first dike builder in ancient times was a skilled engineer named Yu. Over 4000 years ago Yu and countless helpers worked for thirteen years building dikes to prevent the overflow of the Yellow River. His project was a success, and Yu was made emperor. According to Chinese legend, the Yellow River did not flood again for over a thousand years, and Yu became known as Yu the Great.

CHINA

RUSSIA

KAZAKHSTAN

MONGOLIA

INNER MONGOLIA

KYRGYZSTAN

Turpan

XINJIANG

Gobi Desert

Shenyang

N. KOREA

Kashi

TAJIKISTAN

Taklimakan Desert

Yellow

Great

Wall

Beijing

S. KOREA

AFGHANISTAN

PAKISTAN

Kunlun Mountains

NINGXIA

River

Grand Canal

Yellow Sea

Xi'an

Suzhou

Shanghai

Great Himalayan Range

TIBET

River

Wuhan

Hangzhou

East China Sea

NEPAL

Lhasa

Leshan

Yangtze

Chongqing

Mount Everest

BHUTAN

INDIA

BANGLA -DESH

N

Guilin

Xi River

Guangzhou

Taiwan

MYANMAR (BURMA)

VIETNAM

GUANGXI

HONG KONG

Macau

Bay of Bengal

LAOS

Hainan Island

0   500 Kilometers
0   500 Miles

THAILAND

South China Sea

(above) Eleven countries border on China. China's five autonomous regions are located in the border regions.

(below) These people in the Yunnan province rely on the river for washing their clothes.

9

(left) A young Tibetan girl wears a scarf to protect herself from the harsh plateau winds.

(below) After their early morning tai chi chuan exercises, four elderly Han Chinese gather for a chat in a Hangzhou park.

The faces of China

Now that you have explored the landscapes of China, it is time to meet the people who live in this enormous country. The population of China consists of fifty-six nationalities. Most of the people are Han Chinese. These people, who make up ninety-two percent of the population, can trace their **ancestors** back to the time of the Han Dynasty, which ruled China from about 206 B.C. to 220 A.D. The Han share a distinct Chinese **culture**, although they speak different **dialects** of the same language.

A multicultural country

The fifty-five other cultural groups in China total close to sixty million people. They are called "minorities" because, all together, they make up only eight percent of China's huge population. The appearance, clothing, and languages of the **minority** peoples differ dramatically from group to group. This variety in customs and traditions makes China an exciting **multicultural** country.

Autonomous regions

Most of China's minority peoples live in the vast, remote regions in the west and northwest. These areas are known as autonomous regions. The word autonomous means independent. The people are allowed to follow some of their own traditions and cultures but they are governed by China. The five autonomous regions are Tibet, Xinjiang, Inner Mongolia, Guangxi, and Ningxia.

Many people in autonomous regions are not happy being part of China. Tibet, for example, only became part of China because it was taken over by force. China controls all government policies, laws, education, religion, and the media in the autonomous regions. China does not want to grant these regions independence because they provide China with valuable **natural resources**.

(above) These Miao boys are celebrating a festival. Many Miao people live in the southern provinces of Guihou, Yunnan, and Hainan.

(below) This Dai tribeswoman lives in Yunnan Province in southern China. One third of all of China's ethnic minorities live in Yunnan.

China's early history

People have lived in China for hundreds of thousands of years. The bones of a few of the earliest people on Earth have been found there. One of these is Lantian Man, who lived 600,000 years ago; another is Peking Man, who lived around 350,000 years ago.

An ancient civilization

In ancient times, China was ruled by emperors. The Chinese believed that the emperor's right to rule came from heaven. When an emperor died, his title was passed on to a member of his family, usually his eldest son. The son then became the next ruler. A series of rulers from the same family was called a dynasty. The word dynasty also refers to the period of time during which one of these families ruled. During its long history China has been ruled by several dynasties.

Keeping to itself

During most of its ancient history, China had little contact with the rest of the world. The country's rulers felt that the Chinese could not learn anything from other cultures because their own achievements were already far superior. Chinese leaders also feared that outside contact might lead to invasions by foreign powers.

Qin Shi Huang Di was China's first emperor. The Chinese word for emperor means "Son of Heaven."

Famous Chinese dynasties

Here are a few important events and cultural contributions from the reigns of several dynasties:

Zhou (1100–476 B.C.) Confucius and Laotzu, two great Chinese thinkers, lived and wrote. The first canals were built.

Qin (pronounced "Chin") (221–206 B.C.) China took its name from this dynasty. The Great Wall was built.

Han (206 B.C.–220 A.D.) The majority of China's people trace their ancestry back to this dynasty. Paper was invented and **acupuncture** was first used. **Buddhism** came to China from India.

Sui (589–618) The Grand Canal was built.

Yuan (1279–1368) Kublai Khan of Mongolia conquered and ruled. Marco Polo visited China.

Ming (1368–1644) The works of Ming architects, artists, and philosophers earned China the reputation of being the most civilized country in the world. The Forbidden City was built.

Qing (pronounced "Ching") (1644–1911) China saw many changes, including the introduction of the locomotive. The last emperor, Pu Yi, belonged to the Qing dynasty.

The travels of Marco Polo

Although China was not interested in the rest of the world, the world was interested in China. Stories told by a traveler named Marco Polo intrigued the peoples of Europe. In the 1200s Marco Polo and his fellow adventurers traveled by land from Venice, Italy to Cambaluc, China. Marco Polo and his caravan crossed Europe and Asia and traveled along the **Silk Road** north of the Taklamakan Desert. He became friends with Kublai Khan, the Mongolian ruler of China, and stayed in China for seventeen years and returned home with colorful silks and beautiful porcelains.

Trading with the outside world

In the 1500s many countries began to send explorers and traders to China. Soon after, Britain became China's major trading partner. Chinese silks, teas, and porcelain were sold for a great profit in England. To get these treasures, the British traders supplied China with **opium**. A great number of Chinese people became addicted to this dangerous drug. The Chinese fought several wars with the British to stop them from bringing opium into China.

Foreigner takeover

More and more foreign countries wanted control over China and its treasures. China was unable to keep fighting for control over its ports. In 1557 Macau, a small island off the east coast of China, was taken over by Portugal. In 1898 China signed a lease that allowed Britain to take over an area called the New Territories for 99 years. This area included Hong Kong and several other islands.

The return to China

Hong Kong became the world's busiest seaport and the gateway for all goods coming into and going out of China. In 1997 the lease ended and the British government handed Hong Kong back to China. Many Hong Kong citizens were afraid that their lifestyle would change, but the Chinese government agreed to allow Hong Kong to keep its rules and laws for another fifty years. The citizens like their way of life but are also proud to be part of China again. In 1999 Macau was also handed back to the Chinese government.

Hong Kong was under British rule for 99 years. It is now under Chinese rule, and is known as a Special Administrative Region.

Political changes

In the early 1900s many people from other countries were living in China. China feared that it would be divided up into **colonies** belonging to several foreign countries. This angered and threatened the Chinese people.

Father of the country

Sun Yatsen, a doctor, saw that the people of China were poor and unhappy. A small number of rich and powerful people owned all the land, and the peasants did all the work, receiving little for their labors. Dr. Sun Yatsen wanted to help the poor people, so he formed the *Kuomintang*, or the Chinese Nationalist Party. He had many followers because he promised to rid China of all foreign powers and turn over the land to the peasants. In 1911 the nationalists forced the emperor, Pu Yi, to give up the throne. China then became a **democratic** republic, and Sun Yatsen was made president. He is still greatly respected as a national hero. The Chinese call him *kuo-fu*, meaning "father of the country."

The Communist Revolution

Unfortunately, Dr. Sun Yatsen was not able to unite the poor people, and his government could not solve China's many problems. Military commanders, called warlords, seized control of the country. In 1921 the Chinese Communist Party was created, led by a man named Mao Zedong. For almost thirty years the communist and nationalist parties fought against each other for control of the government. Finally, on October 1, 1949 the fighting ended, and Mao announced the formation of the People's Republic of China, a communist state.

What is communism?

Since 1949 China has been a communist country. Communists believe that all resources should be owned by the whole of society. Land, food, and the goods produced by the people are owned by everyone. The government decides what crops are grown on the land, what products are made in factories, and what prices should be charged for goods. It also determines what jobs people have. The communist government plays a big role in the lives of China's citizens. People do not have any say in how they are governed.

Mao Zedong

Mao Zedong, shown left, wanted China to become a strong, independent nation. His communist government set up farming **communes** and sent all children to school. Few foreigners were allowed into China. Mao's plans for modernizing China were unsuccessful. Instead of offering rewards for hard work, Mao wanted people to make many sacrifices. He felt that their hard work should only go towards the good of China. There was little growth in industry or farm production. Nevertheless, the people of China trusted Mao and respected him as the wisest man in China for many years. His picture appeared everywhere, and people carried little red books filled with Mao's words of wisdom.

This Chinese painting illustrates the communist idea. Fishermen are shown pooling their catch to share with the whole village. Through cooperation, more work is accomplished, and people reap greater benefits.

The Cultural Revolution

In 1966 Mao Zedong began a campaign called the Cultural Revolution. He wanted the Chinese people to rebel against authority and old ideas and customs. Unfortunately, things got out of control. This was a difficult time for China. There was a lot of destruction and chaos in the country, and many people were imprisoned. The Cultural Revolution ended in 1969, but it took China many years to recover.

Deng Xiaoping

Shortly after Mao Zedong died in 1976, Deng Xiaoping came to power. He saw that although Mao helped unify the country, China was far from its goal of being a modern industrial nation. Deng began a new system of running the country. He encouraged people to work harder by allowing them to earn extra money by selling crops grown on their land. Within five years the production in China doubled. As part of the new system, China once again began allowing foreigners and new ideas to cross its borders.

Jiang Zemin

Deng Xiaoping died in 1997 leaving Jiang Zemin in power. Jiang has many challenges to face as China's new president. China is changing quickly. People are adjusting to new business practices and new ways of life. Jiang wants China to grow and develop as a modern nation while at the same time keeping a communist system of government.

The democracy movement

Many people in China are not satisfied with their system of government. In June, 1989 thousands of students staged a **protest** in Tienanmen Square in Beijing. They were calling for democracy, which would give them the right to elect their government. The students wanted newspapers and television stations to have the freedom to report the truth. The government put a stop to the protest with gunfire. Hundreds of people were killed and many were thrown in prison. The Chinese people were defeated at Tienanmen Square, but their hope for freedom lives on.

A new way of life

In order to improve the economy in China, the government has been slowly changing the way it runs the country. People are now allowed to start their own businesses. Chinese businesses are allowed to trade with foreign countries. The government is allowing people to own their own land and keep extra wages. As a result, more goods and new products are being developed.

Special Economic Zones

After years of remaining closed to foreigners, China now has an open policy. It encourages other countries to invest money in Chinese businesses. The government has named many coastal towns and cities as Special Economic Zones. In these areas Chinese businesses can form joint ventures with foreign businesses. Joint ventures are businesses that are owned jointly by Chinese and foreign investors.

The responsibility system

For many years China has tried to provide its people with food and jobs. In the early 1980s China encouraged people to make money on their own. This way of making a living was called the responsibility system. Instead of telling people what jobs they should have, the government began allowing people to make their own decisions and incomes. Farmers and small business owners became competitive in the market and the economy prospered.

Free markets

The responsibility system allows farmers to sell their crops at free markets. These markets are not controlled by the government. The farmers are allowed to keep the money they make from their sales. Other merchants can provide services or sell goods that they have made. Barbers, dentists, and outdoor cooks compete for customers at the open markets. Some farmers have made enough money to buy new farming machinery and fertilizers that help improve their crop production.

(left) Hot peppers are sorted at an open market.

(below) A customer makes a deal for fresh vegetables.

Growth spurt

Allowing people to own businesses and encouraging trade with foreign countries helped China's growth. Chinese businesses began to produce iron, cement, textiles, aircraft, television sets, and satellites to sell to foreign countries. Wages and incomes of Chinese workers increased. For the first time, many families could afford items such as motorcycles, television sets, and flush toilets.

Tourism

When foreigners were once again allowed into China, the new tourist industry created many jobs and brought a lot of money into the country. People from all over the world wanted to discover the "new" China. Hotels were built in every major city. The terrible events in Tienanmen Square in 1989 caused the number of tourists visiting China to drop drastically; however, tourism has increased in recent years. China wants to attract more visitors to its cities, historical sites, and cultural festivals.

(top) More Chinese businesses are working with foreign investors than ever before.

(bottom) Car plants are part of China's profitable manufacturing industry.

17

Growing pains

China is experiencing a number of growing pains. Adjusting to a new way of life has been difficult for many people. The responsibility system has increased production, but not everyone is able to make a living. Farmers who do not live in large towns or cities have problems transporting their goods to the free markets. The farmers who make a profit buy machinery that helps them produce more food while employing fewer workers. As a result, many farm workers have lost their jobs and moved to cities to find jobs in factories.

The cost of living

Under the communist system, prices were controlled by the government. Under the new system, the price of food and other goods has risen rapidly. The cost of living has increased faster than the incomes of many people. New employment practices have caused problems in the workplace. Under the old system, everything was shared by members of a work group. Now, managers earn more money than

their fellow workers. Some people think it is unfair that managers earn more money than other employees. The gap between rich and poor people in China is widening.

State-owned enterprises

As a communist country, the Chinese government owned and operated all the businesses in the country. Now, Chinese people and foreign companies are allowed to own businesses. The businesses owned by the government, known as state-owned enterprises, are losing money in the new competitive world of business in China. They borrow money from China's banks but are unable to repay it. This system drains money from the Chinese economy. Many state-owned enterprises are sold to private companies which results in millions of workers losing their jobs.

(above) The sun sets through a haze caused by coal pollution in Beijing. China's cities are experiencing pollution problems due to increased industry.

(above) There is a lack of clean water in China's cities. This woman must wash her vegetables in a polluted river.

Environmental problems

The growth of industry and agriculture in China has created serious environmental problems. There are few laws to stop China's factories from spewing harmful fumes into the air and dumping toxic wastes onto the land and into the water. The Chinese government has promised to solve the pollution problems, but it often puts the country's economic needs first.

Polluted air, land, and water

Using coal is a major cause of air pollution. Most people in China use coal for heating and cooking. Many industries also use coal as their primary source of energy. When coal is burned, it sends out a thick, black cloud of smoke. Household waste is taken to garbage dumps, which are contaminating both the land and the water around them. Wastes such as chemicals, toxic liquids, and sewage are dumped into China's rivers. As a result, many people are experiencing health problems from drinking the water and breathing polluted air.

Changing the landscape

The Chinese government is constructing a dam across the Yangtze river. The Three Gorges Dam will be 1 1/4 miles (2 km) high. It will change the landscape by flooding hundreds of miles of land. Canyons, farmland, and cities will be covered in water. The government is building the dam to create waterways for ships to carry goods to and from the inner regions of China. The dam will create **hydroelectric** power for millions of homes and new factories.

Giant risks

There is a negative side to building such a huge dam. Many people will have to leave their homes when their land is flooded. Hundreds of historic temples and stone sculptures will be lost underwater. Thousands of species of wildlife will lose their natural habitat. Toxic chemicals from abandoned factory sites will pollute the water. Although there will be risks to the environment, the government wants to build the dam to improve the economy.

Food for a billion!

Half the working people in China are farmers. That is a lot of farmers for a country that has little land suitable for farming. Much of China is too steep, too cold, or too dry to support crops.

Fertile plains and basins

Crops grown in China vary from region to region. The plains of northern China are covered with fertile topsoil. This soil, formed from the yellow-gray dust of the Gobi Desert, is rich in lime and holds moisture well. Wheat is the main crop grown on these flat, northern fields. The land also yields good crops of beans, potatoes, cabbages, tomatoes, melons, onions, corn, and millet. Besides these crops, China is the world's largest producer of cotton.

The southeast is China's most productive agricultural region. The fertile Yangtze and Xi river basins are here, and the weather is so mild that crops grow all year round. In a single year a farmer can produce two crops of rice and a third crop of barley or winter wheat. Nearly one half of China's total rice crop is grown in this region. That is why this area is called "China's rice bowl." Peanuts, **lichees**, citrus fruits, sweet peas, sugarcane, and tea are grown in the southeast.

Farming every bit of land

In order to feed such a large population, the Chinese need to farm every bit of land. They plant one type of crop between the rows of another so they will be able to produce as many crops as possible. They even grow food on the sides of roads and railway lines. Some farms are located in the middle of the cities. City farms grow mostly fruit and vegetables, but poultry, pigs, and dairy cows are also raised there.

(left) Terraced fields are cut into hillsides to make more land available for farming rice and vegetables.

(opposite, top) The water buffalo is a valuable work animal.

Hands-on labor

Farming is difficult work in China. Much of the farming is done without the use of modern machinery. Tractors are only used on half the farms in the country. Plowing is often done with wooden plows pulled by oxen or water buffalo. Simple tools such as **sickles**, hoes, and **harrows** aid the farmers with their manual labor. The farmers work hard and put in long days!

Rice farming

Spring is the beginning of the rice-growing season. First, rice seeds are planted in a nursery. While the seeds are sprouting, farmers prepare the rice fields, or paddies. Manure and **nightsoil** are mixed into the soil to make it more fertile. The farmers then build low walls of earth, called dikes, around the paddies so water cannot seep out. Next, the fields are flooded with water. Farmers use a harrow to mix the water with the sun-baked earth.

Plenty of care and water

Planting is usually done by hand. Farmers wade into paddies and place the delicate shoots into the ground one by one. These emerald-green seedling beds need constant care. Paddies must be weeded and the water level checked regularly. As the plants grow, the water level is raised. When the stalks are golden yellow, the rice plants are fully grown and ready to be harvested.

Harvest time

At harvest time the farmers open the dikes and drain the water from the paddies. When the paddies have dried, the rice plants are cut down with sickles. The long stalks are collected, bundled, and laid out to dry. Once dry, the rice grains are removed by hitting the plant. This process is called threshing. The loose grains are collected in sacks and transported to factories. There the shell around each grain is removed. Then the rice is packaged to be sold.

(center) A field worker labors in a wet rice paddy.

(bottom) Farmers ladle water onto vegetables that are grown together on an inner-city farm.

Fishing

Besides growing food on the land, the Chinese also harvest the waters for fish—an important food supply. Along the coastline, people use nets to catch seafood such as mackerel, shrimp, shark, eel, grouper, squid, and crab. Huge nets are cast into the water and dragged along the seabed. One third of a catch is sold; the rest is divided among the crew.

Almost twice as many freshwater fish are caught in China as in any other country in the world. Using poles and nets in the traditional way, people catch some freshwater fish in China's lakes and rivers. Three quarters of all the fish caught in China, however, are raised on fish farms. Fish farms are ponds in which fish such as carp are bred.

Fishers often work into the evening. A fisher balancing on a raft as the sun sets behind the hills of Guilin is a picturesque sight.

Fishing with cormorants

Cormorants are glossy, black birds that dive for fish. These birds are well known for their large appetites. They were used by fishers in many areas of the world until new fishing methods using modern equipment made them unnecessary. The only place where cormorant fishing is still practiced is along the gentle rivers in the south of China. Fishers in these regions use cormorants because the rocky river beds prevent them from using nets.

Diving for fish

Cormorant fishing requires only a few simple tools. These consist of a narrow wooden raft or large tub, a long bamboo pole, and several well-trained cormorants. The fishers use their pole to steer their craft and guide the birds. They splash the water with the pole to encourage the birds to dive. Each bird dives deep and swims underwater until it catches a fish in its beak. Every bird has a leather collar fastened tightly around its neck to prevent it from swallowing the catch. After a cormorant comes back to the raft, the fish is pried from its beak. A dozen trips later its collar is loosened, and the bird is allowed to swallow one fish before going back to work. If the fisher happens to lose count and tries to take the twelfth fish from the cormorant, the bird protests noisily. Not only do cormorants know how to count, they also know their wages!

The cities of China

China's cities are growing and changing rapidly. Forty of them have populations of over a million people. More and more people are moving to the cities to find work. Streets, bicycle paths, markets, and waterways are always crowded.

Beijing, the capital

Beijing is the capital city of China. It used to be called Peking. Beijing is eight hundred years old, but today it is a mixture of old and new. Over the years it has expanded far beyond its old city walls. Many factories have been built on the outskirts of Beijing. The manufacturing of machines, chemicals, agricultural equipment, and textiles are important industries in this city. Beijing is also an important tourist area, receiving thousands of visitors each year.

The Forbidden City

At the heart of Beijing is the Forbidden City, also known as the Imperial Palace. It was built by the Ming emperors in the early 1400s. The palace was called the "Forbidden City" because ordinary people were forbidden to go near its gates. Only government officials and members of the emperor's family were allowed to enter. Today the Forbidden City is open to the public. Its buildings have been converted into museums.

The Venice of the East

The city of Suzhou is a beautiful, old city along the Grand Canal. Suzhou is called the Venice of the East because, like the city of Venice, it is criss-crossed by rivers and canals. People live and trade along the banks, and many families live on *sampans* on the water. A *sampan* is a houseboat with a flat bottom. For centuries Suzhou has been famous for its charming gardens and beautiful silks.

(left) The ancient Grand Canal in Suzhou.

City on the roof of the world

Lhasa, at 11,975 feet (3650 m) above sea level, is the capital of Tibet. Its remote location, fascinating mix of old and new, and the Tibetan people and culture make Lhasa an interesting city. Tibetans are deeply religious people, following **Lama Buddhism**. Monks and nuns dressed in maroon robes are a common sight in Lhasa. Since China took over Tibet in 1949, many Chinese people have moved into the area. Chinese and Tibetan people mingle with tourists from all over the world in Lhasa's streets and markets.

The great port of Shanghai

Shanghai, China's largest city, is a major port. Large amounts of goods are shipped into and out of the country. The name Shanghai means "on the water." Shanghai is China's leader in business and trade. The city has allowed foreign businesses to operate within it since the mid-1800s. For this reason the people of Shanghai have been more exposed to **western** lifestyles than people in other Chinese cities. Shanghai is home to over 13 million people.

(opposite, bottom) Tienanmen Square, the largest public square in the world, is located in Beijing.

(below) The busy port of Shanghai is the most crowded city in China.

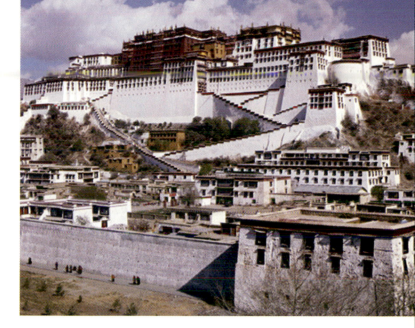

(above) The Potala Palace in Lhasa was once the center of the Tibetan government.

The enchanted hills of Guilin

The city of Guilin is set deep in the mountains of the Guangxi autonomous region in the south of China. Guilin is surrounded by jagged **limestone** peaks and mist-covered valleys of rice fields. Over the centuries the hills have been sculpted by water and wind, producing bizarre shapes and eerie underground caves. These famous hills are the subject of many Chinese paintings. The Chinese people boast that "the best scenery under heaven is found near Guilin." As a result, the city has become a busy tourist center with many hotels and a growing population.

Transportation

People have found many ways to get from place to place in the huge country of China. Travel by water has traditionally been the easiest method of reaching distant locations. Over thousands of years, the Chinese built a vast system of canals to improve the natural travel routes. The most famous of these, the Grand Canal, stretches 1,112 miles (1790 km) from Beijing in the north to Hangzhou in the south. It links five rivers and winds through four provinces. China's many rivers and canals are still crowded with *sampans, junks,* and all kinds of other water vehicles. *Junks* are flat-bottomed sailboats used for carrying cargo.

As well as water "highways," China has extensive train routes, paved roads, and more than two hundred air routes crossing the country. Highways and airways are commonly used to transport cargo, whereas trains remain the most popular mode for travelers.

A Chinese train ride

Train travel is quicker than traveling by bus and less expensive than air travel. There are about 42,255 miles (68 000 km) of train tracks criss-crossing China. Train cars are often overflowing with passengers and their luggage.

There are two ways to travel by train in China: hard seat and soft seat. Hard-seat cars are often crowded. Passengers sit on upright seats that are uncomfortable for long trips. Soft-seat tickets cost more money. The seats are like couches and are more comfortable. There are fewer soft-seat cars available, and these cars are often occupied by Chinese officials and foreign travelers.

(above) This boat is traveling on a city canal in the Eastern province of Jiangsu.

(left) Many Chinese travel within China by train.

(opposite) Millions of people in China use bicycles as their primary source of transportation.

Millions of bicycles

Bicycles are the most popular means of local travel. There are more than three hundred million bicycles in China! At times the streets are clogged with bicyclers. On wider roads special bike lanes are set up with dividers to separate bicycle and motor-vehicle traffic. The most treasured two-wheeled vehicle is the motorbike. So many people want to own motorbikes that their names must be put on long waiting lists.

New car owners

In the past, government officials were among the few people in the country to own automobiles. Today other Chinese residents can buy them, too. When a person wants to buy a car or motorcycle, however, their name is usually put on a waiting list. It may be many months before there is a vehicle available to purchase. With more and more people buying automobiles, many areas in China experience some terrific traffic jams!

The wonders of China

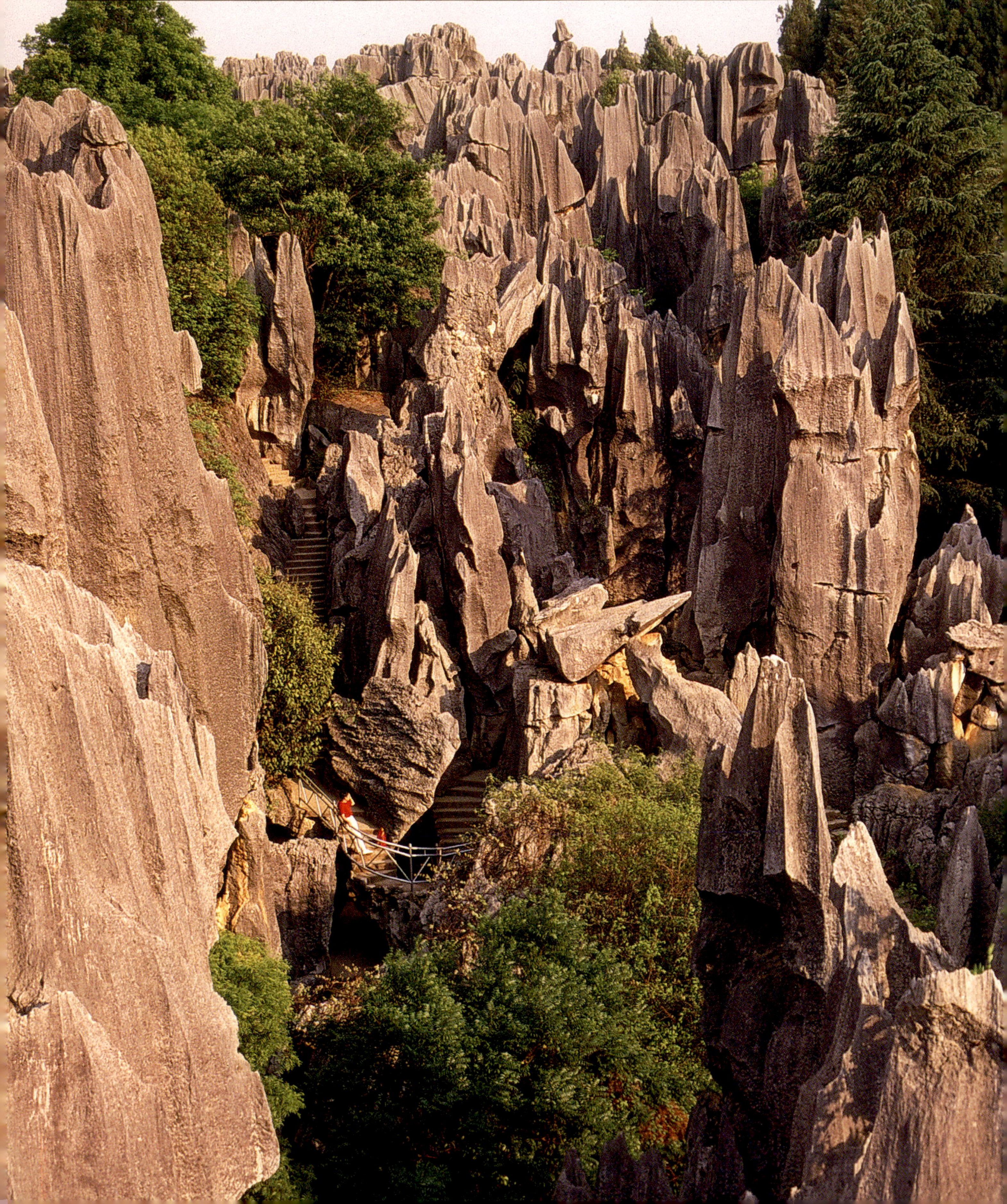

The buried soldiers of Xi'an

Did you know that there is a unique buried treasure in China? Twenty-two centuries ago, life-sized sculptures were buried in the tomb of the first emperor of the Qin dynasty, Qin Shi Huang Di. The sculptures remained undisturbed in this tomb until the twentieth century. When archeologists began to explore old ruins in the city of Xi'an, they discovered the amazing underground army of more than seven thousand **terra-cotta** soldiers as well as real weapons, chariots, and bronze horses. Scientists have restored some of the sculptures that were damaged over time. Others have been left buried in the ground for future archeologists to uncover. Tourists from all over the world travel to Xi'an to see these lifelike soldiers.

The friendship bear

The giant panda has been named one of China's national treasures. Pandas are related to the bear and raccoon families and are only found in the western Sichuan province. China has set up sixteen **nature reserves** for the panda. The largest one is the Wolong Nature Reserve, which is operated with the help of the World Wildlife Fund.

Save the pandas

There are fewer than 1000 pandas left in the world. For more than half-a-million years they roamed the region north and south of the Yangtze River. Pandas eat over twenty-six pounds (12 kg) of bamboo shoots and leaves in a day. Today much of their natural habitat has been destroyed. Many of the native bamboo forests where the pandas lived and found food have been chopped down to make room for farmland and roads. Every 40 to 120 years, large areas of bamboo plants die off. When this happens, many pandas starve to death. Strict laws forbid hunting pandas or cutting down trees that support panda habitats.

(opposite) The Stone Forest attracts visitors who come to see the breathtaking rock formations.

One of the thousands of terra-cotta soldiers found buried in the tomb in Xi'an.

The stone forest

The famous stone forest is located in Yunnan province. This is not a forest of trees. It is a large area of limestone pillars that seem to be growing out of the earth. These limestone formations were pushed up by the shifting earth hundreds of years ago. Powerful currents from underground rivers carved out caves and other fascinating forms in the rock. People climb to the tops of the incredible rock pillars to get a breathtaking view of the surrounding countryside.

The Grand Buddha

The city of Leshan in Sichuan province is the home of the Grand Buddha. This huge sculpture of a seated Buddha is 426 feet (71 m) tall. Construction, which began in the year 713 A.D., took ninety years to complete. The Grand Buddha overlooks three rivers and was built to protect water travelers. Many boating accidents had occurred at the spot chosen for the statue. People hoped the Grand Buddha would watch over them and prevent any further accidents.

The Great Wall

Throughout history many civilizations have built walls to defend themselves against outsiders. By far the most famous of these is the Great Wall of China. The first emperor of China, Qin Shi Huang Di, organized the building of the Great Wall. Building it involved linking together and fixing many walls that already existed from earlier times. As a result, the wall curves and loops through the mountains like a snake.

Back-breaking work!

As you might expect, undertaking such a project was no easy task. Portions of the wall were built on steep mountainsides. Laborers had to struggle to find secure footing. They sweated and strained from dawn until dusk, carrying huge boulders right up to the summits. The boulders were used to construct two thick walls running alongside each other. Tons of earth, lugged in heavy baskets, were dumped in the space between the two barriers. The laborers then pounded the earth into a hard surface with heavy wooden mallets.

*(opposite) Maitraya, or Buddha of the future,
is the name of this statue.*

Landmark Earth

The Great Wall of China is the largest structure in the world. It curves across three provinces and stretches nearly 4,000 miles (6400 km) from Beijing to the deserts of Inner Mongolia. The wall is built on a bed of wide, square stones. Along the way are towers that were used by soldiers watching out for possible attacks. The wall is so wide in some places that several horses can gallop along the top. It is so tall that a person would have to stand on the shoulders of two other people in order to see over it. It is so massive that it is the only structure made by human beings that can be seen from the moon!

A spectacular view

The Great Wall has become a world-famous tourist attraction. People from around the world are amazed by the wall that stretches as far as the eye can see. The view from the wall at dawn and sunset is absolutely spectacular! One day perhaps you will take a walk on the Great Wall or sit on the toes of the Grand Buddha!

Glossary

acupuncture A way of treating illness by stimulating certain pressure points on the body

altitude The height of land above sea level

ancestor A family member from whom a person is descended

Buddhism A religion founded by Buddha, an ancient religious leader from India

civilization A society with a well-established culture that has existed for a long period of time

climate The normal long-term weather conditions for an area

colony An area taken over and controlled by another country

commune A community in which land is held in common, and where members live and work together

contaminate To poison or pollute

culture The customs, beliefs, and arts of a distinct group of people

democracy A type of government in which people elect representatives to make decisions for society

dialect A variation of a language

fertile Able to grow many plants or crops

harrow A horse-drawn farm tool with a heavy frame and disks, used for breaking up plowed land

hydroelectricity Electricity produced by waterpower

Lama Buddhism A religion that combines the teachings of Buddha and the Dalai Lama, the spiritual leader of Tibet

lichee A small round fruit with a brittle red shell and juicy white flesh

limestone A hard type of rock used for building

minority A small group that differs from the larger group of which it is a part

multicultural A term used to describe a society composed of a number of different cultural groups

nature reserve A place where animals and plants can live undisturbed by people

natural resource Anything that exists in nature and is useful to human beings. Forests, mineral deposits, and water are all natural resources.

nightsoil Human waste used as fertilizer

opium An addictive drug

plain A treeless area of land that is flat or nearly flat

protest A public declaration of a complaint or disagreement, often done by a group of people

sea level The average height of the surface of the sea

sickle A curved hand tool that is used for cutting grass, grain, or weeds

Silk Road An ancient road connecting the countries of Europe, the Middle East, and Asia. It was used by traders and travelers.

silt Fine sand or clay that is carried by water and deposited at the mouths of rivers

Special Administrative Region (SAR) An area of China that is run by different social and economic systems than the rest of China.

tai chi chuan A series of body movements used as exercise and to balance one's energy

terra-cotta Hard reddish-brown pottery

western The term used to describe people from the western part of the world, especially Europe and North America, as opposed to people from Asia, such as the Chinese and Japanese

Index

autonomous region 11, 24
Beijing 15, 24, 25, 26, 31
bicycles 24, 27
businesses 16, 17
cars 27
cities 4, 18, 24-25
communism 14, 18
cormorant fishing 23
Cultural Revolution 15
Deng Xiaoping 15
dynasties 11, 12
emporers 12, 24, 31
farming 7, 14, 16, 18, 19, 20-21
fish farming 22
fishing 22-23
flooding 8, 19

Forbidden City 24
free markets 16
Gobi Desert 7, 20
Grand Buddha 29, 31
Grand Canal 5, 24, 26
Great Wall of China 5, 31
Guangxi 11
Guilin 24
Han Chinese 10, 11, 12
Himalayan mountains 5, 6
history 4, 5, 12-13
Hong Kong 13
Inner Mongolia 11, 31
Jiang Zemin 15
Lhasa 24
Mao Zedong 14, 15
Marco Polo 13

Mongolia 7
Mongolian 13
Mount Everest 5, 6, 7
Nepal 5, 6
Ningxia 11
pandas 29
pollution 18, 19
responsibility system 16, 18
rice farming 20, 21
rivers 6, 8, 9, 19, 20, 22, 29
sampans 24, 26
school 14
Shanghai 24, 25
Silk Road 13
Special Administrative Region 13
Special Economic Zones 16

Stone Forest 29
Sun Yatsen 14
Suzhou 24
Taklamakan Desert 5, 7, 13
terra-cotta soldiers 29
terraced fields 20
Three Gorges Dam 19
Tibet 5, 6, 11
Tibetans 10, 24
Tienanmen Square 15, 17, 24
tourists 4, 17, 24, 29, 31
trains 26
travel 26-27
travelers 4
Xi'an 29
Xinjiang 11
Yu the Great 8

4 5 6 7 8 9 0   Printed in the USA   5 4 3